Living Up To Your Name

By Dr. Dennis Corle

Revival Fires! Publishers
P.O. Box 245
Claysburg, PA 16625
(814) 239-2813

copyright 1998 Revival Fires! Publishers
re-printed 2005
ISBN 1-932744-16-9

All Scripture quotations are from the King James Bible.

printed in the United States of America

CONTENTS

What's In A Name?

God has revealed Himself to us in Scripture by a number of characteristic names.

El Shaddai - Almighty God
Adonai - Lord, or Sovereign
Elohim - Strong, faithful, covenant-keeping God
Jehovah-Jireh - The Lord will provide
Jehovah-Shalom - The Lord send peace

The Bible records many more titles that God has chosen to identify Himself and they reveal to us His character and personality. Each of His names portrays a vital attribute of His holy character or a relationship to His people. Though He is identified by many names, there is but one God. So it is with God's people. He has given us a variety of meaningful names, and each one portrays a relationship or character trait that God desires in our lives. Just as the same man could be a husband to his wife, a father to his children, a son to his parents, a brother to his sister, a nephew to his uncle, boss to his employees, etc., there are many names that all apply to us. Not only do these names reveal what we are, but they also challenge us to be what we SHOULD BE. *"I therefore, the prisoner of the Lord, beseech you that ye walk worthy of the vocation wherewith ye are called"* (Ephesians 4:1). As we learn what the Lord has said that we are, and what He says that we should be, we have this challenge - LIVING UP TO YOUR NAME.

By the time you have completed the study of this book, you will have learned some very exciting and interesting things about your new Father, your new family, your new home, and many other marvelous things about being a born-again child of God. The Bible will become much more familiar to you and easier to understand.

Prepare yourself to let the Bible come alive as you learn how you, too, can be living in victory and LIVING UP TO YOUR NAME.

OLD TESTAMENT

Genesis	II Chronicles	Daniel
Exodus	Ezra	Hosea
Leviticus	Nehemiah	Joel
Numbers	Esther	Amos
Deuteronomy	Job	Obadiah
Joshua	Psalms	Jonah
Judges	Proverbs	Micah
Ruth	Ecclesiastes	Nahum
I Samuel	Song of Solomon	Habakkuk
II Samuel	Isaiah	Zephaniah
I Kings	Jeremiah	Haggai
II Kings	Lamentations	Zechariah
I Chronicles	Ezekiel	Malachi

NEW TESTAMENT

Matthew	Ephesians	Hebrews
Mark	Philippians	James
Luke	Colossians	I Peter
John	I Thessalonians	II Peter
Acts	II Thessalonians	I John
Romans	I Timothy	II John
I Corinthians	II Timothy	III John
II Corinthians	Titus	Jude
Galatians	Philemon	Revelation

Lesson #1
Sons Of God

MEMORY VERSE John 1:12 *"But as many as received him, to them gave he power to become the sons of God, even to them that believe on his name."*

The very moment you received Jesus Christ into your heart as your Lord and Saviour, the Bible says that you became a child of God. In John 3:7 Jesus told a man, *"Ye must be born again."* The term *'sons of God'* indicates OUR NEW RELATIONSHIP TO GOD. He has always been our God, but through Christ he has become our heavenly Father, because we have been born spiritually into His family. Prior to this new birth, our family tree was quite different. *"Ye are of your father the devil, and the lusts of your father ye will do. He was a murderer from the beginning, and abode not in the truth, because there is no truth in him. When he speaketh a lie, he speaketh of his own: for he is a liar, and the father of it"* (John 8:44). Now that we have received Christ, to us *'gave he power to become the sons of God . . . '* How blessed we are to be a part of God's own family!

I HAD TO BE BORN INTO THE FAMILY OF GOD.

"Being born again, not of corruptible seed, but of incorruptible, by the word of God, which liveth and abideth for ever" (I Peter 1:23). Suppose I have children. What did they have to do to become my childen? Did they have to earn the right? Did they have to prove themselves worthy? NO! They were born into my family! How long will they be my children? Until they disobey me? No. Until they stop living with me? No. They are not my children because of what they do, but because of who they are. The same applies to us as God's children. We cannot earn the right to be God's children; we must be born into His family. We do not remain God's children because we are good enough, but because

7

we were born into His family. Because we are His children, He will not disown us when we disobey Him, but He will chasten us. Once a person is truly born into the family of God, he can never be 'unborn.' He is forever God's child.

AS A NEWBORN CHILD OF GOD, I HAVE NO PAST.

When a new baby is born, it does not have to 'live down' its past reputation, nor does it have to overcome past memories, past failures, or past sins. A baby has no past. A blessed reality of being born again is that the past is all wiped away. God not only forgives our sin, but He forgets it as well. *"And their sins and iniquities will I remember no more"* (Hebrews 10:17). As newborn children in the family of God, we really can make a fresh start with a clean slate.

I NOW HAVE THE NATURE OF GOD.

"Whereby are given unto us exceeding great and precious promises: that by these ye might be partakers of the divine nature, having escaped the corruption that is in the world through lust" (II Peter 1:4). When we have children, we pass on to them many of our physical characteristics and personality traits. When we are born into God's family, the Holy Spirit comes to live within us and manifests the nature and character of God in our lives. We become more and more like our Heavenly Father. This, of course, causes us to be very different than we were before. *"Therefore if any man be in Christ, he is a new creature: old things are passed away; behold, all things are become new"* (II Corinthians 5:17). Galatians 5:22-23 lists some of these characteristics that the Holy Spirit will manifest in our lives. *"But the fruit of the Spirit is love, joy, peace, long-suffering, gentleness, goodness, faith, meekness, temperance: against such there is no law."*

GOD HAS SPECIAL CARE FOR ME AS HIS CHILD.

"Like as a father pitieth his children, so the LORD pitieth them that fear him" (Psalm 103:13). Just as every father or mother cares for their children, God delights in providing for every need in our lives. *"Therefore take no thought, saying, What shall we eat? or, What shall we drink? or, Wherewithal shall we be clothed? (For after all these things do the Gentiles seek:) for your heavenly Father knoweth that ye have need of all these things. But seek ye*

first the kingdom of God, and his righteousness; and all these things shall be added unto you" (Matthew 6:31-33). God is concerned about every burden of my heart. *"Casting all your care upon him; for he careth for you"* (I Peter 5:7). God wants to hear and answer my prayers. *"And all things, whatsoever ye shall ask in prayer, believing, ye shall receive"* (Matthew 21:22). How wonderful it is to know that God loves me and I am His child. *"Behold, what manner of love the Father hath bestowed upon us, that we should be called the sons of God"* (I John 3:1).

I AM EXPECTED TO OBEY MY HEAVENLY FATHER.

Jesus said in John 14:15, *"If ye love me, keep my commandments."* A parent has the right to expect his child to obey what he says, for he loves the child and has his best interests at heart. God loves us even more than we care about ourselves, and He knows what we need better than we do. So our heavenly Father expects us to be obedient to the commands He has given us.

The first thing I am commanded to do after I become God's child is to be baptized. *"Repent, and be baptized every one of you"* (Acts 2:38). Baptism is the outward picture of what has taken place inwardly, that we have put our trust in the death, burial and resurrection of Jesus to save us. It comes IMMEDIATELY after salvation. *"Then they that gladly received his word were baptized: and the same day there were added unto them about three thousand souls"* (Acts 2:41).

God also commands my membership and faithful attendance in a good, Bible-preaching church. *"Not forsaking the assembling of ourselves together, as the manner of some is; but exhorting one another: and so much the more, as ye see the day approaching"* (Hebrews 10:25).

I am commanded to read my Bible faithfully. *"Search the scriptures; for in them ye think ye have eternal life: and they are they which testify of me"* (John 5:39).

Praying daily is also the command of God. *"Pray without ceasing"* (I Thessalonians 5:17).

God has commanded me to witness and tell others of what He has done in my life. *"But sanctify the Lord God in your hearts: and be ready always to give an answer to every man that asketh*

9

you a reason of the hope that is in you with meekness and fear" (I Peter 3:15).

THE HEAVENLY FATHER WILL CHASTEN DISOBEDIENCE

"And ye have forgotten the exhortation which speaketh unto you as unto children, My son, despise not thou the chastening of the Lord, nor faint when thou art rebuked of him: for whom the Lord loveth he chasteneth, and scourgeth every son whom he receiveth. If ye endure chastening, God dealeth with you as with sons; for what son is he whom the father chasteneth not? But if ye be without chastisement, whereof all are partakers, then are ye bastards, and not sons. Furthermore we have had fathers of our flesh which corrected us, and we gave them reverence: shall we not much rather be in subjection unto the Father of spirits, and live?" (Hebrews 12:5-9).

When God's children disobey Him, He does not disown them, nor does He take away their salvation. They are born into God's family forever. But God does not allow them to live in disobedience and bring shame upon His name and heartache upon themselves. God will CHASTEN a disobedient child, which means the same thing as spanking. Parents do not spank their children because they hate them, but rather because they love them and want them to do what is best and be happy. So God corrects His children because He loves them.

What an honor is ours to be the children of God! It includes many privileges and blessings, as well as responsibilities. How important it is to be OBEDIENT as the sons of God - and be *Living Up To Your Name.*

Did you memorize John 1:12? _____

What have you learned about being a *Child of God*?

10

Lesson #2
Brethren

MEMORY VERSE Psalm 133:1 *"Behold, how good and how pleasant it is for brethren to dwell together in unity!"*

When I was born again as God's child, I acquired a whole new family. The term 'brethren' indicates my NEW RELATIONSHIP TO OTHER BELIEVERS. All of thoses who have put their trust in Jesus Christ to save them as I have are my brothers and sisters in Christ. We have the same Father. We have the same Elder Brother (Jesus). We have the same home where we will spend eternity (Heaven). There should be a special oneness and sweetness among Christians that the unsaved world knows nothing about.

BRETHREN ARE BOUND BY BLOOD.

Just as our brothers and sisters in a family are bound by blood, we are bound to our brethren in Christ by the blood of Jesus, that has paid the debt of our sin. *"Forasmuch as ye know that ye were not redeemed with corruptible things, as silver and gold, from your vain conversation received by tradition from your fathers; But with the precious blood of Christ, as of a lamb without blemish and without spot"* (I Peter 1:18-19).

BRETHREN SHOULD COME TOGETHER AS A FAMILY UNIT TO SPEND TIME WITH ONE ANOTHER AND WITH THEIR FATHER.

Acts 2:42 speaks of ones were just saved and baptized. *"And they continued stedfastly in the apostles' doctrine and fellowship, and in the breaking of bread, and in prayers."* The apostles' doctrine indicates the preaching and Bible teaching that the apostles conducted. Fellowship speaks of the relationship and love between the brethren in the church. The word 'fellowship' carries three basic meanings in the New Testament. First, it

11

speaks of an intimate relationship, such as is enjoyed between a husband and wife. A second usage indicates joint participation in the same work. The third indicates a gift jointly donated. So we find that fellowship is more than just two fellows in the same ship! It is a joint communion, contribution, distribution and communication centered around the Lord Jesus and His work.

Breaking of bread is communion, the second of the two ordinances that Christ gave to the church. (The first is baptism.) Finally, prayer is a vital part of our relationship to the brethren - both prayer *for* the brethren and prayer *with* the brethren. *"Not forsaking the assembling of ourselves together, as the manner of some is; but exhorting one another: and so much the more, as ye see the day approaching"* (Hebrews 10:25). The word "assembling" means 'a called out assembly.' This is what a church is.

BRETHREN SHOULD DEFEND THE CHARACTER OF ONE ANOTHER.

It is important to remember that Christians are not perfect - just forgiven. They do make mistakes. Family members will sometimes disagree with one another, but it does not affect their love for one another. There is a way to show your disagreement without hindering the sweetness of the relationship. Regardless of conflict one with another, family always (or should always) stand together in conflicts with others. They will never yoke up with the enemy against their brother. In speaking of his relationship to other believers, Paul said, *"Who is offended and I burn not."* One of the signs or testimonies that causes others to believe that we are saved is our love for our Christian brethren. *"We know that we have passed from death unto life, because we love the brethren"* (I John 3:14).

Nothing causes grief in the heart of a father or mother more than for the children they love to be feuding and harboring hatred for one another. Our heavenly Father is also grieved if we do not show love to our brothers and sisters in Christ, and nothing pleases Him more than for His children to love one another and be *"together in unity."* As one of the brethren, you have a special place in the family of God in your local church. Your relationship to the rest of the family is vital to your relationship with God. How important it is to be LOVING AND CONCERNED ABOUT OTHER CHRISTIANS - and be *Living Up To Your Name.*

Did you memorize Psalm 133:1? _____

What have you learned about being one of the *Brethren*?

Lesson #3
People Of That Way

MEMORY VERSE   John 14:6   *"Jesus saith unto him, I am the way, the truth, and the life: no man cometh unto the Father, but by me."*

When Christians are referred to as people of "that way," we are being identified with our doctrine, or THE WAY THAT WE BELIEVE. In Acts 19:9; 19:23; 22:4 and 24:22 Christians are called 'People Of That Way.' The world identifies us by what we believe. Our beliefs, of course, are based on the truth of the Word of God. Most folks who say that they believe the Bible do not know what the Bible says. It is important that we know what the Bible teaches concerning the major doctrines or beliefs, and know what we believe.

1. THE VIRGIN BIRTH
This is the teaching that Jesus Christ was born of a virgin mother, Mary, and conceived of the Holy Spirit of God. If Mary had not been a virgin, and Christ had been born of a human father, then He would have been born a sinful man just like any other man, since the sinful nature is passed down through the father's bloodline. But the Bible declares plainly that Jesus Christ was the sinless, perfect Son of God. *"Now the birth of Jesus Christ was on this wise: When as his mother Mary was espoused to Joseph, before they came together, she was found with child of the Holy Ghost"* (Matthew 1:18).
Luke 1:30-35 records some of the conversation between Mary and the angel who announced to her that she would give birth to God's Son. *"And the angel said unto her, Fear not, Mary: for thou hast found favor with God. And, behold, thou shalt conceive in thy womb, and bring forth a son, and shalt call his name JESUS. He*

15

shall be great, and shall be called the Son of the Highest: and the Lord God shall give unto him the throne of his father David: And he shall reign over the house of Jacob for ever; and of his kingdom there shall be no end. Then said Mary unto the angel, How shall this be, seeing I know not a man? And the angel answered and said unto her, The Holy Ghost shall come upon thee, and the power of the Highest shall overshadow thee: therefore also that holy thing that shall be born of thee shall be called the Son of God." Our salvation is dependent on the fact that Jesus is not just a man, but the perfect Son of God that shed His blood for our sin.

2. THE VIRTUOUS LIFE OF CHRIST

Jesus Christ not only was born without sin, but He also lived without sin. "And he that sent me is with me: the Father hath not left me alone; for I do always those things that please him" (John 8:29). Hebrews 4:15 teaches us that Christ had the opportunity to sin, but never did. "For we have not an high priest which cannot be touched with the feeling of our infirmities; but was in all points tempted like as we are, yet without sin."

3. THE VITAL SELF-SACRIFICE OF CHRIST

Jesus Christ willingly came to earth with the intention of living and dying for others. "Even as the Son of man came not to be ministered unto, but to minister, and to give his life a ransom for many" (Matthew 20:28). He chose to make the sacrifices that He made in order to keep us from an eternity in hell.

4. THE VICARIOUS DEATH OF CHRIST

The word 'vicarious' means to take the place of another. "For he hath made him to be sin for us, who knew no sin, that we might be made the righteousness of God in him" (II Corinthians 5:21). "All we like sheep have gone astray; we have turned every one to his own way; and the LORD hath laid on him the iniquity of us all" (Isaiah 53:6). When Jesus died on the cross, he was taking your place, suffering the punishment that you deserve.

5. THE VICTORIOUS RESURRECTION OF CHRIST

"For I delivered unto you first of all that which I also received, how that Christ died for our sins according to the scriptures; And that he was buried, and that he rose again the third day according to the scriptures" (I Corinthians 15:3-4). This is sometimes called 'the Gospel in a nutshell' because it sums up the work of Christ at Calvary. We do not have a Lord and Saviour that is still sealed in a tomb somewhere. Jesus Christ not only died in our place and shed His blood for our sin, but He also rose victorious over death and the grave. *"But now is Christ risen from the dead, and become the first fruits of them that slept"* (I Corinthians 15:20).

6. THE VERY ESSENTIAL INTERCESSION OF CHRIST

Jesus Christ was the God-man, or God in flesh. He was 100% God and 100% man. Because sinful man could not go before a holy God, there had to be a 'go-between,' a mediator or advocate to go to God for us. *"For there is one God, and one mediator between God and men, the man Christ Jesus"* (I Timothy 2:5). Jesus is the only one who can intercede for us before the throne of God. I must come to God through Him. *"Wherefore he is able also to save them to the uttermost that come unto God by him, seeing he ever liveth to make intercession for them"* (Hebrews 7:25).

7. THE VISIBLE RETURNING OF CHRIST

Scripture teaches us that we can expect a two-fold or two-part return of Jesus Christ to the earth. First of all will be the Rapture, when Jesus will come in the clouds FOR HIS SAINTS and receive all of the saved up into Heaven. *"For the Lord himself shall descend from heaven with a shout, with the voice of the archangel, and with the trump of God: and the dead in Christ shall rise first: Then we which are alive and remain shall be caught up together with them in the clouds, to meet the Lord in the air: and so shall we ever be with the Lord"* (I Thessalonians 4:16-17). This will take place before the Tribulation that will come upon all the earth. The Rapture could take place at any time. After the seven-year Tribulation, the Lord will return WITH HIS SAINTS, to defeat the armies of the antichrist. *"And I saw heaven opened, and behold a white horse; and he that sat upon him was called Faithful and True, and in righteousness he doth judge and make war. His eyes were as a flame of fire, and on his head were many crowns; and he had a name written, that no man knew, but he himself. And he was clothed with a vesture dipped in blood: and his name is called The Word of God. And the armies which were in heaven followed him upon white horses, clothed in fine linen, white and clean. And out of his mouth goeth a sharp sword, that with it he should smite the nations: and he shall rule them with a rod of iron: and he treadeth the winepress of the fierceness and wrath of Almighty God"* (Revelation 19:11-15). After this takes place the Millennial Reign of Christ will begin, and He will rule the earth for 1,000 years.

8. THE VERBAL INSPIRATION OF THE SCRIPTURES

II Timothy 3:16, *"All scripture is given by inspiration of God, and is profitable for doctrine, for reproof, for correction, for instruction in righteousness."* The word 'inspiration' means 'God-breathed.' Our Bible is God's message to us, dictated by the Holy Spirit of God to men who wrote exactly what He told them. *"For the prophecy came not in old time by the will of man: but holy men of God spake as they were moved by the Holy Ghost"* (II Peter 1:21).

9. VICTORY ONLY THROUGH CHRIST

Victory over sin, death, hell and the grave is attained for us ONLY by grace through faith in the shed blood of Christ - plus nothing, minus nothing. *"For by grace are ye saved through faith; and that not of yourselves: it is the gift of God: Not of works, lest any man should boast"* (Ephesians 2:8-9). There is absolutely nothing you can do to merit salvation. You must be willing to admit your own unworthiness and trust only in the merit of Christ.

Since you have become a believer in Christ, it is important to be grounded doctrinally - TO KNOW WHAT THE BIBLE TEACHES and be *Living Up To Your Name.*

Did you memorize John 14:6? _____

What have you learned about being one of the *People Of That Way*?

Lesson #4
Saints

MEMORY VERSE Ephesians 5:3 *"But fornication, and all uncleanness, or covetousness, let it not be once named among you, as becometh saints."*

The name 'saint' does not refer to our *perfection,* but to our *position* in Christ. It means ONE WHO IS SET APART. The Corinthian church had a reputation that was a reproach to Christ, and was known for carnality and sin, yet when Paul wrote to them he called them SAINTS, both in I and II Corinthians. *"Paul, an apostle of Jesus Christ by the will of God, and Timothy our brother, unto the church of God which is at Corinth, with all the saints which are in all Achaia"* (II Corinthians 1:1). *"Unto the church of God which is at Corinth, to them that are sanctified in Christ Jesus, called to be saints, with all that in every place call upon the name of Jesus Christ, our Lord, both theirs and ours"* (I Corinthians 1:2). Notice that not only are we called saints positionally because we are saved, but we are called TO BE SAINTS in practice as well.

Every born again believer is a saint. That means that God has set him apart for Himself and His kingdom. *"But God, who is rich in mercy, for his great love wherewith he loved us, Even when we were dead in sins, hath quickened us together with Christ, (by grace ye are saved;) And hath raised us up together, and made us sit together in heavenly places in Christ Jesus: That in the ages to come he might show the exceeding riches of his grace in his kindness toward us through Christ Jesus"* (Ephesians 2:4-7). The Bible teaches us that we are sealed by God's Spirit, just as a document is sealed so that it cannot be changed. *"And grieve not the holy Spirit of God, whereby ye are sealed unto the day of redemption"* (Ephesians 4:30). Our salvation cannot be altered or

21

tampered with; it is settled forever. In God's eyes we already *"sit together in heavenly places in Christ Jesus."* We are as sure of heaven as if we were already there.

Because of the wonderful promises and the grace of God that has made us saints, we should work at fulfilling the implications of the name. We are not saintly to be saved. We should be saintly because we are saved. Every married woman is a wife, and is positionally set apart by marriage to one man. Living up to her name as a wife means that she should be faithful to that man and love him, and be the lady of the house in his home. She then begins to cook and clean and make a comfortable home for him. She does not become a wife by doing these things, but instead, she does these things because she is already a wife.

Not only is it true that we ARE saints in our position because Christ has cleansed us from sin, but we are also CALLED TO BE SAINTS in our practice, living as the Bible teaches that saints should live. It is important, as a saint, that you LIVE A CLEAN AND HOLY LIFE, set apart to God's love and service, and be *Living Up To Your Name.*

Did you memorize Ephesians 5:3? _____

What have you learned about being a *Saint*?

22

Lesson #5
Christians

MEMORY VERSE ACTS 11:26 *"And it came to pass, that a whole year they assembled themselves with the church, and taught much people. And the disciples were called Christians first in Antioch."*

Notice in our memory verse that the believers at Antioch did not call themselves Christians, but they were called Christians by the unsaved world first. The word 'Christian' means 'Christ-one,' 'little Christ,' or a REPLICA OF CHRIST. These folks at the church in Antioch did not just get saved; they continually grew to be more like Jesus until the people around them automatically identified them with Him by their actions.

The name 'Christian' appears only three times in the New Testament. In our memory verse, it is linked to church attendance and doctrine or Bible teaching. They are called 'disciples', which means 'pupils.' Here the Christian is identified by his conduct, character and consistency in serving God. *" . . . And it came to pass, that a whole year they assembled themselves with the church, and taught much people. And the disciples were called Christians first in Antioch"* (Acts 11:26). The second mention of the name is found in Acts 26:28. *"Then Agrippa said unto Paul, Almost thou persuadest me to be a Christian."* In this instance, Paul had shared his testimony of salvation with a man who understood his need of Christ, and yet did not settle the matter of salvation.

The last appearance is in I Peter 4:16 which reads: *"Yet if any man suffer as a Christian, let him not be ashamed, but let him glorify God on this behalf."* This speaks of our conduct amidst suffering and trial. It is an important mark of our identity as 'replicas of Christ,' because He suffered the most agonizing death imaginable, and yet prayed as He died that God would forgive those who were guilty in His death.

In order to live up to our name as a *Christian,* it is vital that we live as Jesus did. The life of Jesus Christ was completely selfless and spent in meeting the needs of others. *"Even as the Son of man came not to be ministered unto, but to minister, and to give his life a ransom for many"* (Matthew 20:28). *"For the Son of man is come to seek and to save that which was lost"* (Luke 19:10). When Jesus saw a blind man He healed him. When He saw a bereaved mother, He raised her son back to life. When He encountered a need that He could meet or a burden He could lighten, He did just that. If we are to be *Christian* in the true sense of the name, we must live as Christ lived - for others.

> *Lord, let me live from day to day*
> *In such a self-forgetful way,*
> *That even when I kneel to pray*
> *My prayer shall be for others.*
>
> *Others, Lord, yes others.*
> *Let this my motto be.*
> *Lord, let me live for others*
> *That I may live like Thee.*

General Booth was a great Christian man who spent his life in helping others and sharing the Gospel. When he became too ill to speak in a scheduled meeting, he was asked to send a telegram message to be read in his absence. When the message was read, it said simply this: "Others. Signed - General William Booth."

Not only in our living, but also in our loving we should be Christlike. He told the disciples that His love for the Father was manifest in His obedience to the Father. *"But that the world may know that I love the Father; and as the Father gave me commandment, even so I do"* (John 14:31). He also identified our love for God with our obedience to Him. *"If ye love me, keep my commandments"* (John 14:15). Our love for others should be Christian as well. Jesus had a heartfelt compassion for people.

24

"But when he saw the multitudes, he was moved with compassion on them, because they fainted, and were scattered abroad, as sheep having no shepherd" (Matthew 9:36). *"But I say unto you, Love your enemies, bless them that curse you, do good to them that hate you, and pray for them which despitefully use you, and persecute you"* (Matthew 5:44). If we have a real love for people, it will be evident in our actions, as it was in the life of Jesus.

In our giving we should be like Jesus as well. *"For ye know the grace of our Lord Jesus Christ, that, though he was rich, yet for your sakes he became poor, that ye through his poverty might be rich"* (II Corinthians 8:9). Jesus left the splendor and glory of His throne in Heaven to come to earth and suffer poverty, shame and death so that we might someday share Heaven with him. How much more should we be willing to sacrificially give whatever we can so that others may also be saved. Paul commended the Christians in Macedonia for their exemplary manner in giving. *"For to their power, I bear record, yea, and beyond their power they were willing of themselves; Praying us with much intreaty that we would receive the gift, and take upon us the fellowship of the ministering to the saints. And this they did, not as we hoped, but first gave their own selves to the Lord, and unto us by the will of God"* (II Corinthians 8:3-5). Jesus sacrificed everything He had, and gave His life for us. We should be Christlike in our giving to Him.

As Christians, we are being identified as 'little Christs,' or copies of the Original. If you were brought to trial as a Christian, would there be enough evidence to convict you? It is vitally important to be LIKE CHRIST in the way that we live and in every area of life - and be *Living Up To Your Name.*

Did you memorize Acts 11:26? _____

What have you learned about being a *Christian?*

Lesson #6
Disciples

MEMORY VERSE Matthew 16:24 *"Then said Jesus unto his disciples, If any man will come after me, let him deny himself, and take up his cross, and follow me."*

Our name *disciple* refers to a DISCIPLINED PUPIL OR AN APPRENTICE, one who is receiving 'on-the-job' training' from the Master. It indicates learning by doing. As *disciples* we are to be learning at the feet of Jesus, paying close attention to His every word, and following closely the instruction that he has given. We must realize, however, that this learning is not just an accumulation of facts, but an incorporation of those facts into our daily lives. It is not just a knowledge of the head, but also a knowledge of the heart, hands and feet. In other words, a lesson is not a well learned if it is not well-lived. A truth learned is a truth applied. A real disciple lives what he learns.

This kind of learning takes discipline and character, as the name implies. Doing what is right is not always fun, it is not always popular, it is not always easy. But it is always right. The important things in the Christian life take character and discipline. Church attendance takes discipline. Giving takes discipline. Soulwinning takes discipline. Separation from sin takes discipline. For a time a new believer can run on the emotion and excitement of being saved, but without warning the new will wear off and then it takes discipline to continue being faithful at what God wants us to do. For some new converts the unsignalled slack in their zeal is as sudden and dramatic as a car running out of gas. They had no warning that serving Christ would ever be less exciting than the day they were saved, just like young couples are the day they are married. At this point it is important to be determined to do right because it is right, and not for any other

27

reason.

This is not to say that serving the Lord will never be happy or exciting again. On the contrary, the Christian life is the most joyful, exciting life possible. Being what God created us to be is the happiest existence we can know. But a person who has decided to remain faithful to Christ as long as it is fun and easy will soon be disillusioned, just like the person who will remain married as long as it is fun and easy. There are certainly going to be a few bad days, and a few trying circumstances. But for those who have purposed to obey the Lord no matter what, the Christian life will continually grow sweeter and more rewarding. *"But as it is written, Eye hath not seen, nor ear heard, neither have entered into the heart of man, the things which God hath prepared for them that love him"* (I Corinthians 2:9).

Throughout the Gospel accounts of the life of Christ, there is a silent but evident division between the multitudes and the disciples. "The multitudes" always refers to the crowds of people who thronged Jesus when it was to their personal benefit. They listened to the teachings of Jesus and enjoyed the blessings of His miracles when He fed them and healed their sicknesses. The disciples remained with Jesus even in storms and persecutions. *"And he was in the hinder part of the ship, asleep on a pillow: and they awake him, and say unto him, Master, carest thou not that we perish? And he arose, and rebuked the wind, and said unto the sea, Peace, be still. And the wind ceased, and there was a great calm"* (Mark 4:38-39). They not only listened to His teachings; they also lived by His teachings. They not only benefited from His miracles, they participated in His miracles. *"And Jesus took the loaves; and when he had given thanks, he distributed to the disciples, and the disciples to them that were set down; and likewise of the fishes as much as they would"* (John 6:11). They not only received the Gospel of salvation but they also shared it with others. *"And they went out, and preached that men should repent"* (Mark 6:12).

Jesus gave the identifying marks of disciples. The first is love. *"By this shall all men know that ye are my disciples, if ye have love one to another"* (John 13:35). Love is an action word, not

28

just an emotion. It is doing what is best for another no matter what the personal expense. Another mark is obedience to the Word of God. *"Then said Jesus to those Jews which believed on him, If ye continue in my word, then are ye my disciples indeed; And ye shall know the truth, and the truth shall make you free"* (John 8:31-32). The third identifying characteristic is sacrifice and unselfishness. *"And whosoever doth not bear his cross, and come after me, cannot be my disciple"* (Luke 14:27). The Lord is to come first, before family or anything else that is important to us, if we are to be disciples. *"If any man come to me, and hate not his father, and mother, and wife, and children, and brethren, and sisters, yea, and his own life also, he cannot be my disciple"* (Luke 14:26). The Lord was not teaching that we should hate our loved ones and ourselves, but rather that our love for Him should so far exceed all other loves that they would seem like hate by comparison. He makes this plain in Matthew 10:37. *"He that loveth father or mother more than me is not worthy of me: and he that loveth son or daughter more than me is not worthy of me."* Fruit is another identifying mark of a disciple, and the fruit of a Christian is souls. *"Herein is my Father glorified, that ye bear much fruit; so shall ye be my disciples"* (John 15:8).

Disciples are those who are living what they learn, and who discipline themselves to live according to the Word of God even when it is not easy. As a disciple of Christ, it is important to be COMPLETELY COMMITTED to Him - and be *Living Up To Your Name.*

Did you memorize Matthew 16:24? _____

What have you learned about being a *Disciple?*

29

Lesson #7
Ambassadors For Christ

MEMORY VERSE II Corinthians 5:20 *"Now then we are ambassadors for Christ, as though God did beseech you by us: we pray you in Christ's stead, be ye reconciled to God."*

The title we are given as *Ambassadors For Christ* indicates our REPRESENTATION OF CHRIST IN THIS WORLD. Just as an American ambassador goes to another country as a representative of the people in America, so we are not here in this world to represent ourselves or our own views, but to exemplify Christ to the world. Paul said in this verse that we are representing Christ, and God speaks through us to share the gospel with others. We are here in the place of Christ, or instead of Christ.

The representation that we provide to the world will determine their view of Christ and Christianity. This is why it is so important that every part of our life be wholly consecrated to the Lord. *"Whether therefore ye eat, or drink, or whatsoever ye do, do all to the glory of God"* (I Corinthians 10:31). In light of this truth, we need to pause in every situation to determine exactly how Jesus would act or react, and then do that which exemplifies and glorifies Him. What an honor and responsibility is ours to be His ambassadors!

Notice first of all that an ambassador is one who is in a foreign land. *"For our conversation is in heaven; from whence also we look for the Saviour, the Lord Jesus Christ"* (Philippians 3:20). The word used here for conversation is also translated as 'citizenship.' When we are saved, we also become citizens of Heaven, and our life in this world is in a strange land - this is not our final home. Hebrews 11 records many Bible characters who demonstrated great faith, and says of them in verse 13: *"These all died in faith, not having received the promises, but having seen them afar off, and were persuaded of them, and embraced them, and confessed that they were strangers and pilgrims on the earth."* Verse 16 says, *"But now they desire a better country, that is, an heavenly: wherefore God is not ashamed to be called their God: for he hath prepared for them a city."* Because we are children of God, our home is in Heaven and we are out of place in this world. We are in this world but not of this world. God's purpose for us here is that we should be representatives of Christ and of our heavenly homeland.

"Then spake Jesus again unto them, saying, I am the light of the world: he that followeth me shall not walk in darkness, but shall have the light of life" (John 8:12). Jesus described our representation of Himself in Matthew 5:14-16. *"Ye are the light of the world. A city that is set on an hill cannot be hid. Neither do men light a candle, and put it under a bushel, but on a candlestick; and it giveth light unto all that are in the house. Let your light so shine before men, that they may see your good works, and glorify your Father which is in heaven."* Jesus is the light of the world and we are lights in this world. We should always reflect the views and character of Jesus Christ as a mirror reflects the light that shines upon it. *"That ye may be blameless and harmless, the sons of God, without rebuke, in the midst of a crooked and perverse nation, among whom ye shine as lights in the world"* (Philippians 2:15). The important thing is never what others think of us, but what they think of Jesus because of us.

The moon has no light of its own, but it reflects the light of the sun that shines upon it. When the earth comes between the sun and the moon, it causes a lunar eclipse, and the moon cannot be seen because the light of the sun is being blocked by the earth. In the same way, Christians experience a 'spiritual eclipse' if they allow the world and worldliness to come between them and the Lord. They no longer reflect the light of Christ before the world because it is blocked out by worldliness. *"Love not the world, neither the things that are in the world. If any man love the world, the love of the Father is not in him"* (I John 2:15). 'The world' does not refer to the globe, but to the things of this world that are lasting. Sometimes the world comes between Christ and Christians by way of materialism and love for money, or a love for sin. A man named Demas allowed a 'spiritual eclipse' to take place in his life because of love for the world. *"For Demas hath forsaken me, having loved this present world, and is departed unto Thessalonica"* (II Timothy 4:10). A second illustration of a spiritual eclipse took place in Matthew 26, when Peter allowed a desire for popularity and acceptance to cause him to deny the Lord. When a 'spiritual eclipse' takes place in a person's life, he no longer reflects the light of Christ to the world, and the world cannot see Christ in him as God intends for them to do.

The world can come between the Lord and us and cause a spiritual eclipse to take place through three major areas in our lives: (1) our ACTIONS; (2) our ATTITUDES; and (3) our ASPIRATIONS. We rightly represent Christ to this world by our actions when we obey His Word and do what He would do if He were here in our place. *"But be ye doers of the word, and not hearers only, deceiving your own selves"* (James 1:22). Our attitude, as well, should be like Christ's. *"Let this mind be in you, which was also in Christ Jesus: Who, being in the form of God, thought it not robbery to be equal with God: But made himself of no reputation, and took upon him the form of a servant, and was made in the likeness of men: And being found in fashion as a man, he humbled himself, and became obedient unto death, even the death of the cross"* (Philippians 2:5-8). Finally, our aspirations should correspond with those of Jesus. *"And he was withdrawn from them about a stone's cast, and kneeled down, and prayed, Saying, Father, if thou be willing, remove this cup from me: nevertheless not my will, but thine, be done"* (Luke 22:41-42). Our aspiration ought to be only to do the will of our Heavenly Father.

It is important that we share Christ with others not only in what we say but in how we live. Statistics prove that you will remember only 70% of what you hear three hours later and only retain 10% of that in three days. You will remember 72% of what you see three hours later and retain only 20% in three days. But when you can both see and hear, you will remember 85% after three hours, and 65% after three days. Our witness to others ought to be visible as well as spoken. As an *Ambassador For Christ* it is important to recognize the responsibility to be a REPRESENTATIVE OF CHRIST TO THE WORLD - and be *Living Up To Your Name.*

Did you memorize II Corinthians 5:20? _____

What have you learned about being an *Ambassador For Christ?*

Lesson #8
Fishers Of Men

MEMORY VERSE Matthew 4:19 *"And he saith unto them, Follow me, and I will make you fishers of men."*

Jesus spoke to Peter and Andrew who were fishermen by trade, and challenged them as He challenges and commands us to be soulwinners. Our name, *Fishers Of Men*, has to do with OUR OCCUPATION OR PURPOSE IN THIS WORLD - bringing men and women to Jesus Christ. He made a declarative statement that if we were to follow Christ, we would definitely become fishers of men. Therefore, if we are not fishing, we are not really following Him. Soulwinning is not a talent or a gift for a select group of people. It is the command of God for every born again believer. In Luke 5:10 Jesus spoke to James and John who had also made their living as fishermen. To them He said, *"Fear not; from henceforth thou shalt catch men."*

The Lord has commissioned us to take the gospel to those around us, and tell others how to be saved. *"Go ye therefore, and teach all nations, baptizing them in the name of the Father, and of the Son, and of the Holy Ghost: Teaching them to observe all things whatsoever I have commanded you: and, lo I am with you alway, even unto the end of the world. Amen"* (Matthew 28:19-20). It has been said, "It's a funny thing. When you fish for fish, they are alive until you catch them and then they die, but when you fish for men they are spiritually dead until you catch them and then they have eternal life!" We have the great privilege and responsibility of sharing the gospel with others, and winning souls to Christ.

If you spend any time around fishermen, you will no doubt hear them discussing the kind of bait they use. What do we use to fish for men? *"For I am not ashamed of the gospel of Christ: for it is the power of God unto salvation to every one that believeth; to the Jew first, and also to the Greek"* (Romans 1:16). The gospel is simply the wonderful truth that Jesus Christ gave Himself to die for our sins, was buried, and rose again on the third day in victory over sin and death. I Corinthians 15:3-4 is sometimes called 'the gospel in a nutshell.' *"For I delivered unto you first of all that which I also received, how that Christ died for our sins according to the scriptures; And that he was buried, and that he rose again the third day according to the scriptures."* The gospel, 'the power of God unto salvation,' is given to us so that we may be able to use it to fish for men.

Fishermen also spend a lot of time discussing where to fish, and no doubt those who make the biggest catch know where to find the best fishing holes. Where should we fish for men? *"And he said unto them, Go ye into all the world, and preach the gospel to every creature"* (Mark 16:15). The entire world is our fishing hole! But where should we start? Before He ascended back to Heaven, Christ told all of the believers to begin in their own city, sharing the gospel with their own immediate family and neighborhood first. From there they were to spread out to the areas around them until their outreach went to the entire world. *"But ye shall receive power, after that the Holy Ghost is come upon you: and ye shall be witnesses unto me both in Jerusalem, and in all Judea, and in Samaria, and unto the uttermost part of the earth"* (Acts 1:8).

Everyone knows that the best part of any fishing story is always the big catch. Just the same, the most exciting thing about soulwinning is the people who get saved. *"For whosoever shall call upon the name of the Lord shall be saved"* (Romans 10:13). A fisherman is not satisfied just to spread bait, or just to get a fish on the hook, but is determined to catch them and get them into the boat. We should not be satisfied just to spread the gospel or pass out gospel tracts, but also be determined to get people saved, baptized and serving God in the local church, as the entire commission instructs us. Fishing for men is much more than just living the lifestyle; it is laboring in bringing people to Christ. We can have a part in people missing Hell and going to Heaven, and in their hearts and lives being changed. One of the greatest joys of being saved is the opportunity to share it with others.

In order to be a fisher of men, simply ask the person to whom you are speaking, "Do you know for sure that if you died today that you would go to Heaven? If you could know that for sure, you would want to, wouldn't you? Would you be willing to let me show you how the Bible says that we can know for sure we will go to Heaven?" If they agree, turn to Romans 5:12. *"Wherefore, as by one man sin entered into the world, and death by sin; and so death passed upon all men, for that all have sinned."* We have all inherited a sinful nature. God says that we 'all have sinned.' The only penalty or price that will pay for sin is DEATH. This includes a physical death and a SPIRITUAL death also. (Turn to Revelation 21:8.) *"But the fearful, and unbelieving, and the abominable, and murderers, and whoremongers, and sorcerers, and idolaters, and all liars, shall have their part in the lake which burneth with fire and brimstone: which is the second death."* This verse describes the spiritual death as a lake that burns with fire and brimstone - HELL! According to the Bible, if we die in our sins we will have to go to hell.

Revelation 20:12, *"And I saw the dead, small and great, stand before God; and the books were opened: and another book was opened, which is the book of life: and the dead were judged out of those things which were written in the books, according to their works."* If we would die in our sin, we would also have to face God with everything we have ever said wrong, thought wrong, or done wrong. But God loved us so much that He made a way that our sin could be paid for without you and I going to Hell. (Turn to John 3:16.) *"For God so loved the world, that he gave his only begotten Son, that whosoever believeth in him should not perish, but have everlasting life."* Jesus paid the price of our sins for us when He died on the cross, was buried and rose again. (Turn to John 1:12.) *"But as many as received him, to them gave he power to become the sons of God, even to them that believe on his name."* If we want our sin to be forgiven then we must RECEIVE JESUS and the payment He made for our sin. The Bible promises that if we will receive Him, He will make us a child of God.

Ephesians 2:8-9 says, *"For by grace are ye saved through faith; and that not of yourselves: it is the gift of God: Not of works, lest any man should boast."* Salvation is a free gift offered to us, because Jesus has already paid the price for it. When someone offers you a gift, all you must do for it to be yours is to receive it. The Bible says that receiving Jesus is as simple as opening the door. (Turn to Revelation 3:20.) *"Behold, I stand at the door, and knock: if any man hear my voice, and open the door, I will come in to him, and will sup with him, and he with me."* He promised that if we would sincerely invite Him into our hearts, 'I WILL come in.' Are you willing to claim His promise and invite Jesus to come into your heart right now?

You Forgot My Soul

You lived next door to me for years;
  We shared our dreams, our joys and tears.
A friend to me you were indeed,
  A friend who helped me when in need.
My faith in you was strong and sure,
  We had such trust as should endure.
No words between us could impose;
  Our friends were like - and so, our foes.

What sadness, then, my friend, to find
  That, after all, you weren't so kind;
The day my life on earth did end
  I found you weren't a faithful friend.
For all those years we spent on earth,
  You never talked of second birth.
You never spoke of my lost soul
  And of the Christ Who'd make me whole.

I'm lost today eternally
  And tell you now my earnest plea.
You cannot do a thing for me -
  No words today my bonds will free.

But do not err, my friend, again -
Do all you can for souls of men.
Plead with them not quite earnestly,
Lest they be cast into hell with me.

General Booth was once asked to sign King Edward VII's Bible. In it he wrote: "Some men's ambition is art; Some men's ambition is fame; Some men's ambition is gold; My ambition is the souls of men." What a great privilege and responsibility is ours to share the message of Christ's death, burial, and resurrection for sin so that others might believe and be saved. How important it is as *Fishers Of Men* TO BE WITNESSING TO ALL THOSE AROUND YOU - and be *Living Up To Your Name*.

Did you memorize Matthew 4:19? _____

What have you learned about being a *Fisher Of Men?*

You may order New Testaments marked for soulwinning and other helpful soulwinning tools from:
Dennis Corle Evangelistic Association
RD 1 Box 940
Claysburg, PA 16625
(814) 239-2813

Lesson #9
Soldier

MEMORY VERSE II Timothy 2:3-4 *"Thou therefore endure hardness, as a good soldier of Jesus Christ. No man that warreth entangleth himself with the affairs of this life; that he may please him who hath chosen him to be a soldier."*

When a person receives Christ into their heart, it will not be long before they realize they are right in the middle of a fierce battle. Before they were saved, the devil had no reason to oppose them, but now that they are Christians, he will go to every measure and method to hinder them from serving the Lord and from spreading the gospel message. Our name *Soldier* has to do with OUR WARFARE AGAINST SATAN. We need to become familiar with the battle plan and equip ourselves for the struggle.

THE ARMY HAS A CAUSE. When David saw the army of Israel trembling in fear before their enemy, he demanded of them, *"Is there not a cause?"* (I Samuel 17:29). David's understanding of the cause made him courageous to fight in the face of overwhelming odds because He knew it was the cause of God and that God would fight for him. Our cause is the gospel that has been entrusted to us by the Lord. *"Beloved, when I gave all diligence to write unto you of the common salvation, it was needful for me to write unto you, and exhort you that ye should earnestly contend for the faith which was once delivered unto the saints"* (Jude 3). There is a great cause for our mission, because the gospel is the only hope of salvation for men and women who will otherwise perish in Hell.

THE ARMY HAS A LEADER. Our Commander-In-Chief has given us leaders under Himself who are directly answerable to Him, and who pass on to us the orders He has given. *"And he gave some, apostles; and some, prophets; and some evangelists,* and some, pastors and teachers; For the perfecting of the saints, for the work of the ministry, for the edifying of the body of Christ" (Ephesians 4:11-12). Our pastor is responsible to God to tell us what God expects from us, and to lead us as a band of soldiers in obeying those orders. Imagine an army on the battlefield composed of all privates and no commanding officers. Everyone would be racing about in confusion with no common battle plan and no cooperation or teamwork, probably shooting at their own army. The result would be certain defeat. In the same way, it is necessary that God place someone in leadership over us as soldiers of Christ, so that we may band together and follow orders as a unit.

THE ARMY HAS ARMOR AND WEAPONRY. *"Finally, my brethren, be strong in the Lord, and in the power of his might. Put on the whole armour of God, that ye may be able to stand against the wiles of the devil. For we wrestle not against flesh and blood, but against principalities, against powers, against the rulers of the darkness of this world, against spiritual wickedness in high places. Wherefore take unto you the whole armour of God, that ye may be able to withstand in the evil day, and having done all, to stand. Stand therefore, having your loins girt about with truth, and having on the breastplate of righteousness; And your feet shod with the preparation of the gospel of peace; Above all, taking the shield of faith, wherewith ye shall be able to quench all the fiery darts of the wicked. And take the helmet of salvation, and the sword of the Spirit, which is the word of God: Praying always with all prayer and supplication in the Spirit, and watching thereunto with all perseverance and supplication for all saints"* (Ephesians 6:10-18). Our faith, truthfulness and righteous living, as well as our salvation, are all very real protections for us spiritually. Although Satan's darts are hurled at us continuously, they cannot penetrate this spiritual armor to harm us. The important factor in its protection, though, is constant use. The moment our guard is down, the devil will be quick to spot our weakness and make a surprise attack that will mean certain defeat. There is never a moment when it is not important to put on the whole armor of God.

The purpose of armor, of course, is not so that we can stand protected as a target for the enemy to shoot at. Its purpose is so that we can actively fight against the enemy, skillfully using the weapons at hand. Our primary weapon is the sword of the Spirit, the infallible, inerrant Word of God. We should know how to use it in defeating the enemy, and also in rescuing those captives who are held in his power. The Bible is ours to love, to study, to meditate upon and to use in the battle. By constant use we become more capable of using it effectively. Prayer is also a very powerful force by which to conquer the foe. Though we are powerless in ourselves to conquer, we have open communication to the All-powerful Who will instantly come to our aid. In having our feet shod with the preparation of the gospel of peace, we have the message of deliverance to those held in bondage to the enemy and the mission of snatching them from the burning brands of Hell.

In II Corinthians 10:3-5, we are given some information about our weaponry. *"For though we walk in the flesh, we do not war after the flesh: (For the weapons of our warfare are not carnal, but mighty through God to the pulling down of strongholds;) Casting down imaginations, and every high thing that exalteth itself against the knowledge of God, and bringing into captivity every thought to the obedience of Christ."* This is the very powerful and available equipment that is needed to win in this spiritual warfare.

THE ARMY HAS A UNIFORM. When two armies meet on the battlefield and the soldiers in the front lines hold hand-to-hand combat with the enemy, there is never a problem in distinguishing friend from foe. The reason for the clear and instant distinction is the uniform. In the Lord's army, we ought to be immediately recognizable as Christians. We ought to look like, act like, and dress like the Bible says Christians should. Anything in our appearance that hints of wickedness or worldliness should be changed without a question. *"And be not conformed to this world: but be ye transformed by the renewing of your mind, that ye may prove what is that good, and acceptable, and perfect, will of God"* (Romans 12:2).

An illustration from Spurgeon's Gems points out the problems of refusing to be recognizable as a soldier of Christ. "What would her Majesty think of her soldiers if they should swear they were loyal and true, yet were to say, 'Your Majesty, we prefer not to wear these regimentals; let us wear the dress of civilians! We are right honest men and upright, but do not care to stand in your ranks, acknowledged as your soldiers; we had rather slink into the enemy's camp and into your camps, too, and not wear anything that would mark us as being your soldiers!' What must the Lord think of those who belong to Him, yet refuse to be identified as His?"

One identifying factor that people immediately notice about us is our clothing, and the Bible is clear about what kind of clothing we should wear. *"The woman shall not wear that which pertaineth unto a man, neither shall a man put on a woman's garment: for all that do so are abomination unto the LORD thy God"* (Deuteronomy 22:5). Again in I Timothy 2:9-10, Christian clothing is defined. *"In like manner also, that women adorn themselves in modest apparel, with shamefacedness and sobreity; not with broided hair, or gold, or pearls, or costly array; But (which becometh women professing godliness) with good works."* The words 'modest apparel' are defined as 'a long flowing garment.' Ladies are not to be bold or loose in their actions or their dress, and are to avoid extremes in hairstyles, jewelry, and clothing. Any clothes that hint of unisex or sensuality are clearly unacceptable.

Hair is another important factor in appearance. *"Doth not even nature itself teach you, that, if a man have long hair, it is a shame unto him? But if a woman have long hair, it is a glory to her: for her hair is given her for a covering"* (I Corinthians 11:14-15). God has set the standard for us, that short hair identifies masculinity and long hair signifies femininity. For us to discard these Bible guidelines in appearance is willful disobedience to God's standard. The story is told of a man during the Civil War who feared for his life. He decided to wear a blue jacket and grey breeches, hoping that it would portray him as a neutral figure. Contrary to what he had intended, both armies fired on him, thinking him to be the enemy. Compromise never pays.

THE ARMY HAS AN ENEMY. *"Be sober, be vigilant;*

because your adversary the devil, as a roaring lion, walketh about, seeking whom he may devour" (I Peter 5:8). In the same measure with which God loves us and seeks our good, the devil so vehemently hates us and seeks our destruction. But he is the original liar, and tries to make us believe he is on our side and seeks to give us something good and enjoyable. All of the devil's traps are wrapped in pretty packages, but we find out too late that they aren't at all what they seemed to be. Sin always takes you farther than you want to go, keeps you longer than you want to stay, and costs you more than you're willing to pay.

Ecclesiastes 8:8 tells us that there is no discharge from fighting this war; it is a life-long conflict. *"There is no man that hath power over the spirit to retain the spirit; neither hath he power in the day of death: and there is no discharge in that war; neither shall wickedness deliver those that are given to it."* James 4:7 gives us the central key to victory against our enemy, the devil. *"Submit yourselves therefore to God. Resist the devil, and he will flee from you."* In order to win against Satan, we must first be totally submitted to God in obedience and service. If we are submitted to the Lord, we can then resist the devil and he will have to flee in defeat. While every soldier that is drafted will go to battle, only those who go beyond the call of duty will receive a medal of honor.

"Victory is the result of orders being obeyed rather than discussed," a great general once said. *"But thanks be to God, which giveth us the victory through our Lord Jesus Christ"* (I Corinthians 15:57). *"Now thanks be unto God, which always causeth us to triumph in Christ, and maketh manifest the savour of his knowledge by us in every place"* (II Corinthians 2:14). We are assured the victory in this battle if we only obey orders. How important it is as soldiers to be OBEDIENTLY AND ACTIVELY CONTENDING FOR THE FAITH and be *Living Up To Your Name.*

Did you memorize II Timothy 2:3-4?

What have you learned about being a *Soldier?*

Lesson #10
Sheep

MEMORY VERSES John 10:27 *"My sheep hear my voice, and I know them, and they follow me."*

Jeremiah 23:3-4 *"And I will gather the remnant of my flock out of the countries whither I have driven them, and will bring them again to their folds; and they shall be fruitful and increase. And I will set up shepherds over them which shall feed them: and they shall fear no more, nor be dismayed, neither shall they be lacking, saith the LORD."*

The Lord often uses the name *Sheep* to speak of us, and when He does so, it refers to OUR RELATIONSHIP TO THE PASTOR WHICH IS HIS UNDER-SHEPHERD, AND TO THE LOCAL CHURCH, which is our fold. Sheep are very dumb and helpless animals, and desperately need the care and protection of a shepherd. And whether we want to admit it or not, we need the help of a man of God. Although it is true that the Lord is the Good Shepherd, The Great Shepherd, and the Chief Shepherd, it is evident from our text that He has chosen to set under-shepherds over us called pastors.

In Jeremiah 23:3 the Lord promises to gather His sheep. This illustrates His saving grace at work in drawing us to Himself in salvation. He then says that He will bring them to their folds (plural). It is plural because it is not only talking about the conversion but the appointed place of protection and provision that God has provided for that particular sheep, his church. When the sheep are in their fold they are fruitful and increase in number. This has to do with my responsibility in soulwinning. However, I will not be fruitful if I am not in the fold that the Lord has appointed for me.

In verse four He promises to set shepherds over us. The word for 'shepherd' would carry much the same idea as the word 'pastor' is understood to convey. Both the shepherd and the pastor have the job of comforting, protecting, feeding, and leading their flock. Jesus identifies Himself to us as our Good Shepherd Who was willing to sacrifice His life to save us from harm. *"I am the good shepherd: the good shepherd giveth his life for the sheep"* (John 10:11). He said that the identifying characteristics of His sheep were faith and obedience. *"But ye believe not, because ye are not of my sheep, as I said unto you. My sheep hear my voice, and I know them, and they follow me"* (John 10:26-27). Let us make some observations.

EVERY SHEEP HAS A FOLD. *"Praising God, and having favour with all the people. And the Lord added to the church daily such as should be saved"* (Acts 2:47). Although there might be many flocks of sheep, and none of them 'bad' flocks, there is only one to which a particular sheep belongs. That is his home, a place of belonging and security and provision. So it is with us as sheep. The Good Shepherd that laid down His life for us intends that we settle into the home church or 'flock' where He places us and follow Him faithfully there. We do not need to switch to another flock because that shepherd is feeding at our favorite pasture this week. We need to faithfully follow the shepherd that God has given to love and care for us with the flock He has placed us in, and our spiritual needs will be met as God intends.

EVERY SHEEP HAS A SHEPHERD. In Hebrews 13 the Lord gives us instruction concerning our shepherds, and describes them as, 'those who have the rule over us.' In verse seven He says, *"Remember them which have the rule over you, who have spoken unto you the word of God: whose faith follow, considering the end of their conversation."* In verse 17 He gives further instruction concerning our relationship with our pastor. *"Obey them that have the rule over you, and submit yourselves: for they watch for your souls, as they that must give account, that they may do it with joy, and not with grief: for that is unprofitable for you."* Finally in verse 24 He gives another command to the sheep. *"Salute all them that have the rule over you, and all the saints."*

48

We are to REMEMBER them that have the rule over us. Notice that it is not dictatorship but rulership. Second we are to RESPOND to those who have the rule over us. There are two reasons for this. The first is the fact that they are watching for our souls, and the second is because they must give account as undershepherds. Finally we are to RESPECT those who have the God-given rule over us. We should not be on a first name basis with our pastor, for the old saying is true, 'Familiarity breeds contempt.' Though your pastor is no better than you, God has placed him in a position of leadership and responsibility. He does pull rank on you, in the same way that the general pulls rank over the private though they are both equal as men.

I have had the privilege to watch shepherds at work on several occasions, and by so doing have learned some valuable lessons. The shepherd is totally dedicated to the welfare of the sheep regardless of the cost. The sheep on the other hand express complete trust in and followship toward the shepherd. So it is with us. We are to respond to the pastor that God has given us just as we would respond to the Lord Jesus Christ Himself.

In Matthew 10:40-41 He illustrates this truth. *"He that receiveth you receiveth me, and he that receiveth me receiveth him that sent me. He that receiveth a prophet in the name of a prophet shall receive a prophet's reward; and he that receiveth a righteous man in the name of a righteous man shall receive a righteous man's reward."*

STRAYING SHEEP ARE IN DANGER. A sheep that has wandered away from his fold and from his shepherd faces grave danger and peril for which he has no defense in himself. We are exhorted to *"Be sober, be vigilant; because your adversary the devil, as a roaring lion, walketh about, seeking whom he may devour"* (I Peter 5:8). Just as a wandering sheep is subject to attack by lions and other dangerous predators, when we leave the spiritual protection that God has provided through our church and our pastor, we are vulnerable to the attack of Satan, who seeks to destroy us.

As God's *Sheep,* it is important that you REMAIN FAITHFUL TO YOUR LOCAL CHURCH, FOLLOW THE LEADERSHIP

OF YOUR PASTOR - and be *Living Up To Your Name.*

Did you memorize John 10:27 and Jeremiah 23:3-4?

What have you learned about being God's *Sheep?*

Lesson #11
Stewards

MEMORY VERSE I Corinthians 4:2 *"Moreover, it is required in stewards, that a man be found faithful."*

An important truth for us to grasp in this life is that we have nothing of ourselves. *"The earth is the Lord's, and the fulness thereof; the world, and they that dwell therein"* (Psalm 24:1). Everything we have, everything we do, and everything we are was given to us by God, so we must please Him by the way in which we handle these affairs. Our name *Stewards* signifies our ACCOUNTABILITY TO GOD CONCERNING EVERYTHING HE HAS GIVEN US.

In Bible times, a steward was the most trusted servant in a household. He was wise and diligent in the handling of goods and finances, yet nothing that he cared for was his own. He did this on behalf of his master in his master's absence. God calls us stewards so that we may be reminded that nothing we have is really our own. It was all given to us by a loving heavenly Father, and we must answer to Him for the way it is used or wasted. Job realized that he had nothing in himself. *"And said, Naked came I out of my mother's womb, and naked shall I return thither: the LORD gave, and the LORD hath taken away; blessed be the name of the LORD"* (Job 1:21). Anything that we would have to leave behind at death or the Rapture we cannot truly call our own. It is simply 'on loan' to us, and we are responsible to God for what we do concerning it.

WE ARE STEWARDS OF OUR TIME. The most valuable thing that all of us possess is certainly time. Just ask someone who doesn't have much time left, and they will tell you that they would gladly give anything and everything that they have in exchange for time. Time is life, and life comes from God, so we are to wisely use and invest our time for His glory. *"See then that*

51

ye walk circumspectly, not as fools, but as wise, Redeeming the time, because the days are evil" (Ephesians 5:15-16). Redeem means 'to buy back,' and we are instructed to 'redeem' the time God has given us, not squandering the hours, but carefully investing each precious one in tasks that are equal in value. When the Lord said, "Occupy till I come," He meant to 'go into business' in His absence. INVEST your time in eternity rather than SPENDING it selfishly.

WE ARE STEWARDS OF OUR TREASURE. *"Beware that thou forget not the Lord thy God, in not keeping his commandments, and his judgments, and his statutes, which I command thee this day . . . And thou say in thine heart, My power and the might of mine hand hath gotten me this wealth. But thou shalt remember the Lord thy God: for it is he that giveth thee power to get wealth, that he may establish his covenant which he sware unto thy fathers, as it is this day"* (Deuteronomy 8:11, 17-18). Although we are clearly accountable to God for what we do with 100% of the finances He gives to us, He has given a clear command concerning the first 10% of everything we acquire. This is a tithe. *"Will a man rob God? Yet ye have robbed me. But ye say, Wherein have we robbed thee? In tithes and offerings. Ye are cursed with a curse: for ye have robbed me, even this whole nation. Bring ye all the tithes into the storehouse, that there may be meat in mine house, and prove me now herewith, saith the Lord of hosts, if I will not open you the windows of heaven, and pour you out a blessing, that there shall not be room enough to receive it"* (Malachi 3:8-10). The tithe, or the first ten percent, belongs to the Lord before it ever reaches my hand. I am clearly instructed to give it back to Him to meet the needs of His house, the local church. Above my tithe, I am instructed to give the Lord offerings. A tithe proves that I am honest and do not rob God. An offering proves my love for Him. *"Give, and it shall be given unto you; good measure, pressed down, shaken together, and running over, shall men give into your bosom. For with the same measure that ye mete withal it shall be measured to you again"* (Luke 6:38). We are stewards in the area of money.

WE ARE STEWARDS OF OUR TALENT. Every ability that

the Lord has blessed me with He expects me to use for His glory - *"For unto whomsoever much is given, of him shall be much required"* (Luke 12:48). Just as a multi-millionaire has more to give account to God for in the area of finances than someone who is poor, so a person whom God has given special talent or ability is accountable to God for how it is used, abused, or neglected. God has given special abilities to be used in special ministries and tasks. Let us be diligent to find and to finish the task the Lord has for each of us.

WE ARE STEWARDS OF OUR CHILDREN. *"Lo, children are an heritage of the LORD: and the fruit of the womb is his reward"* (Psalm 127:3). Our children are a priceless trust that the Lord has graciously 'loaned' to us for a few years, in the confidence that we will nurture and train them to love and serve Him with their entire lives. *"Train up a child in the way he should go, and when he is old, he will not depart from it"* (Proverbs 22:6). Our godly and scriptural training of our families has such great potential to bring honor and glory to Him. This is a valuable treasure that God has entrusted to us as His stewards - our children.

WE ARE STEWARDS OF OUR PHYSICAL BODIES. *"What? know ye not that your body is the temple of the Holy Ghost which is in you, which ye have of God, and ye are not your own? For ye are bought with a price: therefore glorify God in your body, and in your spirit, which are God's"* (I Corinthians 6:19-20). The Bible is clear that we are accountable to God for the bodies in which we dwell. *"Know ye not that ye are the temple of God, and that the Spirit of God dwelleth in you? If any man defile the temple of God, him shall God destroy; for the temple of God is holy, which temple ye are"* (I Corinthians 3:16-17).

WE ARE STEWARDS OF THE GOSPEL. *"But as we were allowed of God to be put in trust with the gospel, even so we speak; not as pleasing men, but God, which trieth our hearts"* (I Thessalonians 2:4). When a trust fund is set up, it is in care of a steward or trustee. That individual is bound to use that fund for the best interest of the person it was meant for, not for himself. So also, we are trusted with the gospel of salvation that Christ died

53

for the sins of the whole world so that they could trust in Him and be saved. This gospel has been placed in our trust, and it is our responsibility to see that it reaches those for whom it is provided. We are accountable to God as stewards of the gospel message to see that it is given to the lost world so that they will have the opportunity of salvation. We will answer to Him for how we accomplish or fail as His stewards with this precious treasure.

We are accountable to God for our stewardship. *"And he said also unto his disciples, There was a certain rich man, which had a steward; and the same was accused unto him that he had wasted his goods. And he called him, and said unto him, How is it that I hear this of thee? give an account of thy stewardship; for thou mayest be no longer steward"* (Luke 16:1-2). An insubordinate employee who will not do as he should with his employer's goods will be put out of that stewardship and be fired. If we are found unfaithful in any area for which we are accountable, we may be put out of the stewardship. This could mean losing our health, our life, our wealth, our children, our ability to serve, etc. As God's *Steward,* it is important that you BE FAITHFUL IN DOING EXACTLY WHAT HE HIMSELF WOULD DO WITH WHAT HE HAS ENTRUSTED TO YOU, and be *Living Up To Your Name.*

> *Only one life*
> *Twill soon be past*
> *Only what's done*
> *For Christ will last.*

Did you memorize I Corinthians 4:2?

What have you learned about being a *Steward?*

Lesson #12
Kings And Priests

MEMORY VERSE Revelation 1:5-6 *"And from Jesus Christ, who is the faithful witness, and the first begotten of the dead, and the prince of the kings of the earth. Unto him that loved us, and washed us from our sins in his own blood, and hath made us kings and priests unto God and his Father; to him be glory and dominion for ever and ever. Amen."*

This exciting passage in Revelation reveals two important names that the Lord has given us. The name Priest has to do with OUR HIGH PRIESTLY PRIVILEGES AND RESPON-SIBILITIES OF PRAYER AND SERVICE TO GOD. The name King has to do with OUR FUTURE GLORY OF RULING AND REIGNING WITH CHRIST. What an important position has been granted to us as kings and priests with God!

In the Old Testament, the high priest was the only person who was entitled to enter the Holy of holies within the temple, and thus into the very presence of God. He did so to sacrifice and make atonement for the sins of all the people, and to intercede to God in prayer for them. In the New Testament we each have access to the Holy of holies, because of Christ's sacrifice of Himself for our atonement. *"Having therefore, brethren, boldness to enter into the holiest by the blood of Jesus, By a new and living way, which he hath consecrated for us, through the veil, that is to say, his flesh; and having an high priest over the house of God; Let us draw near with a true heart in full assurance of faith, having our hearts sprinkled from an evil conscience, and our bodies washed with pure water. Let us hold fast the profession of our faith without wavering; (for he is faithful that promised;)"* (Hebrews 10:19-23). The Book of Hebrews was written to the Jews to prove to them that Jesus Christ and the New Testament did not contradict

55

or eradicate the Old Testament, but simply fulfilled it. Hebrews 4:16 also assures us that we may 'come boldly' into His presence. *"Let us therefore come boldly unto the throne of grace, that we may obtain mercy, and find grace to help in time of need."*

As priests we have access to the throne of grace, and an audience with the God of Heaven. It is our privilege and responsibility to intercede in prayer, not only for our own needs, but for the souls and the needs of others. A great preacher, R.A. Torrey, said, "Talking to men for God is a great thing, but talking to God for men is greater still. One will never talk well and with real success to men for God who has not learned well how to talk to God for men." *"Confess your faults one to another, and pray one for another, that ye may be healed. The effectual fervent prayer of a righteous man availeth much"* (James 5:16). The great apostle Paul prayed fervently for the salvation of his Jewish people. *"Brethren, my heart's desire and prayer to God for Israel is that they might be saved"* (Romans 10:1). It is our blessed duty to prayerfully give sacrifice and service to the Lord of lords.

While our name *PRIESTS* has to do with our present ministry, our name *KINGS* has to do with our future exaltation, that of reigning with Christ in His Millennial kingdom. The parable Jesus gave concerning the talents pictures us facing Christ at the end of life with what we have done or failed to do for Him. In it, the obedient servants received reward for their faithful service, part of which was rulership. *"His lord said unto him, Well done, thou good and faithful servant; thou hast been faithful over a few things, I will make thee ruler over many things: enter thou into the joy of thy lord"* (Matthew 25:21).

We are now living in the age of grace, which shall soon come to a close when the Lord appears to rapture us. Then the Bible teaches us that there will be a seven year Tribulation period upon the earth, while we are in Heaven with the Lord, followed by a one thousand year Millennium, in which the Lord will return with His saints (us) to rule and reign on the earth. It is during this time that we will receive the reward of rulership, and it is according to our faithfulness.

THERE IS REMEMBRANCE FOR SERVING CHRIST. Just

imagine the glow on the servant's face as his Master speaks the words, *"Well done, thou good and faithful servant."* The Lord will remember and commend our faithful labor for Him. *"For God is not unrighteous to forget your work and labour of love, which ye have shewed toward his name, in that ye have ministered to the saints, and do minister"* (Hebrews 6:10).

THERE IS REWARD FOR SERVING CHRIST. The Bible tells us of five crowns that will be awarded to those who have excelled in the service of Christ.

*The crown of glory - I Peter 5:4
*The crown of righteousness - II Timothy 4:8
*The crown of life - James 1:12; Revelation 2:10
*The crown of rejoicing - I Thessalonians 2:19
*The crown of reward for endurance - I Corinthians 1:25

THERE IS ROYALTY BESTOWED FOR SERVING CHRIST. We are royalty, not only as children of God and heirs with Christ, but also as rulers in that coming kingdom. *"Blessed and holy is he that hath part in the first resurrection: on such the second death hath no power, but they shall be priests of God and of Christ, and shall reign with him a thousand years"* (Revelation 20:6).

THERE IS REMORSE FOR UNFAITHFULNESS IN SERVING CHRIST. Every Christian who shirks his duty and dishonors his Lord will someday face Him, ashamed and remorseful. *"And now, little children, abide in him; that, when he shall appear, we may have confidence, and not be ashamed before him at his coming"* (I John 2:28).

We have an important position, both now and in the time to come, now in service and then in reigning with Him. As Kings And Priests, it is important that we BE FAITHFUL IN PRAYER AND IN SACRIFICIAL SERVICE to our Lord - and be *Living Up To Your Name.*

Did you memorize Revelation 1:5-6?

What have you learned about being *Kings and Priests?*

Lesson #13
Servant

MEMORY VERSE Romans 6:22 *"But now being made free from sin, and become servants of God, ye have your fruit unto holiness, and the end everlasting life."*

The primary word for servant in the New Testament is *doulos,* signifying one that is born into the service of his master rather than one captured and sold into slavery. This name is said to denote' one that is in a permanent relation of servitude to another, his will altogether swallowed up in the will of the other.' When the Lord calls us by the name Servant, it refers to our COMPLETE SURRENDER TO HIS WILL AND HIS WORK. We were not captured against our will and forced into slavery, but rather were set free from slavery to sin in this new birth by which we are born into the service of the house of God. We, too, should allow our will to be completely swallowed up by God's will, and our love for Him to be manifested in faithful and obedient service to Him.

"Know ye not, that to whom ye yield yourselves servants to obey, his servants ye are to whom ye obey; whether of sin unto death, or of obedience unto righteousness? But God be thanked, that ye were the servants of sin, but ye have obeyed from the heart that form of doctrine which was delivered you. Being then made free from sin, ye became the servants of righteousness. I speak after the manner of men because of the infirmity of your flesh: for as ye have yielded your members servants to uncleanness and to iniquity unto iniquity; even so now yield your members servants to righteousness unto holiness. For when ye were the servants of sin, ye were free from righteousness. What fruit had ye then in those things whereof ye are now ashamed? for the end of those things is death. But now being made free from sin, and become servants to God, ye have your fruit unto holiness, and the end everlasting life.

For the wages of sin is death; but the gift of God is eternal life through Jesus Christ our Lord" (Romans 6:16-23). As long as we remained in service to sin, the only payment we received in return was spiritual death, and the death of everything that is dear to us. But God gives to His servants spiritual life, and every good and precious thing to enjoy.

There is a choice involved for the servant. I cannot choose if I will serve, because everyone is either a servant of God or a servant of the devil. But I do have the choice of whom I will serve. *"And if it seem evil unto you to serve the LORD, choose you this day whom ye will serve; whether the gods which your fathers served that were on the other side of the flood, or the gods of the Amorites, in whose land ye dwell: but as for me and my house, we will serve the LORD"* (Joshua 24:15). If we are truly the servants of God, it will be evident not only in what we say, but also in what we do. *"His mother saith unto the servants, Whatsoever he saith unto you, do it"* (John 2:5). The Lord questions the lip service that is not followed through by obedience. *"And why call ye me, Lord, Lord, and do not the things which I say?"* (Luke 6:46).

There are four kinds of servants. The first is the servant who does only what he wants to do. *"In those days there was no king in Israel: every man did that which was right in his own eyes" (Judges 21:25).* When we fail to acknowledge the authority of the Lord in our lives, we will slip into the habit of doing what seems alright to us, rather than what God has commanded us to do. *"There is a way that seemeth right unto a man, but the end thereof are the ways of death" (Proverbs 16:25).*

The second servant is the one who obeys when it is convenient and easy to do so. "If it's not too hot or too cold, if I'm not too tired or too sick, if the task is not too hard or unpleasant, then I'll be glad to do what God says." In John 6, Jesus' preaching did not set well with some of those that considered themselves His servants. *"Many therefore of his disciples, when they had heard this, said, This is an hard saying: who can hear it?" (John 6:60).* They decided, like many people do, that they would turn back and not serve the Lord anymore. *"From that time many of his disciples went back, and walked no more with him" (John 6:66).*

A missionary in Africa was once asked if he really liked what he was doing. His response was shocking. "Do I like this work?" he said. "No. My wife and I do not like dirt. We have reasonably refined sensibilities. We do not like crawling into vile huts through goat refuse . . . But is a man to do nothing for Christ he does not like? God pity him, if not. Liking or disliking has nothing to do with it. We have orders to 'Go,' and we go. Love constrains us." We, too, must go beyond what is convenient or enjoyable if we are to be servants of God. *"For unto you it is given in the behalf of Christ, not only to believe on him, but also to suffer for his sake"* (Philippians 1:29).

The third kind of servant is the one who does all that is commanded him. *"So likewise ye when ye shall have done all those things which are commanded you, say, We are unprofitable servants: we have done that which was our duty to do"* (Luke 17:10). This is the servant who is completely loyal, faithful, and obedient, who does even the hard tasks that are given to him. He obeys every order that he clearly understands his master to give him. The obedient servant of the Lord is one who is baptized, faithfully attending a Bible-preaching church, praying, reading his Bible, tithing his income, separating from things he knows are sinful, and trying to win others to Christ.

Yet there is still a fourth kind of servant. The servant who obeys every command is still called an unprofitable servant. The fourth, or profitable servant, is the one who goes beyond the call of duty and does more than could be expected of him. He is often called 'The Second Mile Christian.' During New Testament times, the Jewish people were under the rule of the Roman Empire. If a Roman soldier commanded a Jewish citizen to carry his load for him, the law stated that he must carry it one mile. However, Christ exhorted believers to demonstrate their spirit of servitude by going beyond the requirements. *"And whosoever shall compel thee to a mile, go with him twain"* (Matthew 5:41). He was forced to go the first mile, but the second mile he chose to go, and thus he could show his Christianity by his willingness to do more than just what was expected of him. If we are to be profitable servants to God, then we must obey ALL of what He commands us to do, and then go even beyond what is expected.

As *Servants*, it is important to be TOTALLY SURRENDERED TO GOD'S WORK AND GOD'S WILL and be *Living Up To Your Name.*

Christ has no hands but our hands to do His work today;
He has no feet but our feet to lead men in His way;
He has no tongue but our tongue to tell men how He died;
He has no help but our help to bring them to His side.

We are the only Bible the careless world will read;
We are the sinner's gospel, We are the scoffer's creed;
We are the Lord's last message, given in deed and word;
What if the type is crooked? What if the print is blurred?

What if are hands are busy with other work than His?
What if our feet are walking where sin's allurement is?
What if our tongues are speaking of things His lips would spurn?
How can we hope to help Him and hasten His return?

-- Anniel Johnson Flint

Did you memorize Romans 6:22?

What have you learned about being a *Servant*?